Grow, Crow!

amicus readers

Mankato, Minnesota

by Marie Powell

Ideas for Parents and Teachers

Amicus Readers let children practice reading informational texts at the earliest reading levels. Familiar words and concepts with close photo-text matches support early readers.

Before Reading
- Discuss the cover photo with the child. What does it tell him?
- Ask the child to predict what she will learn in the book.

Read the Book
- "Walk" through the book and look at the photos. Let the child ask questions.
- Read the book to the child, or have the child read independently.

After Reading
- Use the word family list at the end of the book to review the text.
- Prompt the child to make connections. Ask: *What other words end with -ow?*

Amicus Readers are published by Amicus
P.O. Box 1329, Mankato, MN 56002
www.amicuspublishing.us

Copyright © 2014. International copyright reserved in all countries. No part of this book may be reproduced in any form without written permission from the publisher.

Library of Congress Cataloging-in-Publication Data

Powell, Marie, 1958-
  Grow, crow! / Marie Powell.
    pages cm. -- (Word families)
  ISBN 978-1-60753-515-7 (hardcover) -- ISBN 978-1-60753-543-0 (eBook)
  1. Reading--Phonetic method. 2. Readers (Primary) I. Title.
  LB1573.3.P694 2013
  372.46'5--dc23
                    2013010401

Photo Credits: Ivan Galashchuk/Shutterstock Images, cover; G Tipene/Shutterstock Images, 1; Alena Brozovo Shutterstock Images, 3; Shutterstock Images, 4, 12; SuperStock, 7; Alexander Chelmodeev/Shutterstock Images, 9; Arto Hakola/Shutterstock Images, 10, 11; Pa Reeves Photography/Shutterstock Images, 15

Produced for Amicus by The Peterson Publishing Company and Red Line Editorial.

Editor Jenna Gleisner
Designer Marie Tupy
Printed in the United States of America
Mankato, MN
12-2013
PO1186
10 9 8 7 6 5 4 3 2

The winter **snow** melts in spring. A mother **crow** builds a nest.

4

The wind may **blow**,
but the nest is safe.
The baby **crow** hatches
from its egg.

The mother feeds her baby **crow**. It will **grow** bigger every day.

The young **crow** cannot fly yet. It looks out at the **meadow**.

The **crow** hops out
of the tree. Look out

below, **crow**!

The **crow** lands on a **low** branch. Its parents will **show** the **crow** how to flap its wings.

It might be **slow**, but the **crow** will **grow** and learn to fly. **Grow, crow!**

Word Family: -ow

Word families are groups of words
that rhyme and are spelled the same.

Here are the -ow words in this book:

below
blow
crow
grow
low
meadow
show
slow
snow

Can you spell any other words
with -ow?